BE AN
OVERCOMER...
EVEN IF YOU HAVE
TO DO IT
SEVERAL TIMES

Jill Dorman

ISBN 978-1-63903-910-4 (paperback)
ISBN 978-1-63903-911-1 (digital)

Christian Faith Publishing, Inc.
832 Park Avenue
Meadville, PA 16335
www.christianfaithpublishing.com

Printed in the United States of America

To my dear cousin Laura Muteti
Her never-give-up attitude, her positivity, and her love for others
is an excellent example of how we all should be. She fought a
very courageous battle with breast cancer. She is our true hero!

November 1, 2019, 3:45 p.m.
Grocery parking lot on the pharmacy end, three spaces down (first one
past the handicap space), facing west

I remember it vividly. I was unloading groceries from my cart into the car. That's where I was when my world turned upside down.

1

THREE LETTERS...W, H, Y

Why? How many times a day do you ask that question? Being a fifth grade teacher, I'm sure I ask it more than the average person. Why did you just push him? Why don't you have a pencil? Why aren't you in line? Why are you talking? Why are you putting your shoelace in your mouth? Why is your desk wet? On the same token, if you have kids of your own, you know how many times they ask *why* questions on an average day. If you don't know, the answer is up to two hundred times! It's the nature of being a human to wonder about things and want to know the reasoning behind things. I may not be a child, but I can tell you that I've asked the question *why* close to two hundred times a day myself in recent years, and honestly, I still don't have an answer.

You see, my family's journey with cancer began over ten years ago in 2009. My sister-in-law, Amy McLaughlin, was diagnosed with cancer shortly after the birth of my nephew, Nathan. Amy was my older brother Jeremy's wife.

As she went through her journey, the family was in shock and disbelief but also lost in all the lingo and jargon that comes along with fighting cancer. Many times, I questioned God. Why was he doing this to my brother? Why was he doing this to our family? We went to church every Sunday growing up. We were in the youth group. I played the piano and organ for church services. We were what were considered good people. So why were we chosen to deal with this?

Amy was one of those people who were nice to everyone. She had her opinions, but she didn't force them on others. Being new to the cancer world, our family was not really sure what to do to help her and Jeremy. So we did what family does; we surrounded her with love and did what we could to lighten the load. My mom organized a party of sorts to show our support of Amy. We showed up in matching shirts and spent the day pampering Amy and enjoying laughs together. We had a huge turnout for the event including Amy's friends and coworkers.

Right after Thanksgiving in 2010, Amy's condition worsened. While many were preparing for Christmas with their families, we were preparing for the passing of our loved one. In her last days, I was helping my brother by staying at the house with the kids. Abby was three, and Nate had just turned one in October. Amy was not well at the time, and I had decided I didn't want to see her in that condition. I wanted to remember her as the happy, smiley sister-in-law I knew, not the one currently bald due to chemo, hooked up to wires and machines to keep her alive. To this day, I don't regret that decision. Amy knew I loved her, and she knew I was taking care of her babies so that Jeremy could be at the hospital with her.

On one particular night when I was staying with the kids, we were watching TV, and the show *Frosty the Snowman* came on. Abby, who was three at the time, wanted to watch it. While this seemed like a seemingly innocent request, it turned out to be something that would stick with me for the rest of my life.

Have you ever had a song play that instantly flooded your memory of a situation from the past? Or maybe it's a scent that when you smell it, you remember something from your childhood. I'm sure that "Frosty the Snowman" is probably not one of those songs you would think of as a tearjerker that would send memories flooding back to you. But that night, watching Frosty, I ended up crying through the whole show. That show took on a whole new meaning to me that night. Have you ever really listened to the words in "Frosty the Snowman"?

> Frosty the Snowman
> Was alive as he could be
> And the children say
> He could laugh and play
> Just the same as you and me.
>
> Frosty the Snowman
> Knew the sun was hot that day
> So he said let's run
> And we'll have some fun
> Now before I melt away.
>
> Frosty the Snowman
> Had to hurry on his way
> But he waved goodbye
> Saying don't you cry
> I'll be back again someday.

Prior to the diagnosis, Amy was alive as she could be. She laughed and played with her kids just like any parent should. But after she was diagnosed, Amy knew she didn't have a lot of time left, so she did everything she could to try to keep the kids' lives as normal as possible. Even though it exhausted her, she did her best to make memories with them, knowing there was a chance they would never even remember her because they were so young. But if there is one thing Amy wouldn't want, it would be people crying that she was gone. She knew one day we would be reunited again. To this day, I cannot hear that song without thinking of Amy and all the other cancer patients who had seemingly normal lives before all of that melted away. They waved goodbye and said, "Don't you cry. I'll be back again someday."

Sadly, Amy passed away on December 16, 2010, just nine days before Christmas. She had a husband, a three-year-old daughter, and a fourteen-month-old son at the time. I vividly remember Amy's mom coming back to the house after being at Kohl's, getting some clothes for the funeral. She said something that has stuck with me all these years. She said, "All those people at the store were hustling and bustling, pushing and shoving, cutting in line, trying to find the perfect Christmas gift for their loved ones, and there I was trying to find the perfect outfit to bury my daughter in." She was so right! Do you ever stop and think about the people around you at the store, at the doctor's office, at a restaurant? We have absolutely no idea what is going on in other people's lives, and because of that, we just need to be kind.

While the days leading up to the funeral as well as the funeral itself are a bit of a blur to my memory, I vividly remember a seemingly innocent request by my three-year-old niece. When we were getting ready to leave the funeral home after the calling hours, my brother was holding Abby up near the casket. She innocently asked, "Daddy, can we wake Mommy up now?" This was about the time I really started questioning God. I had a lot of *why* questions. Why were my niece and nephew denied the chance to be raised by their mother? Why was Amy denied the chance to be their mother? Why did God punish some people this way?

My oldest brother, Jeremy, with Amy, Abby, and Nate on
Halloween 2010, just a few months prior to her passing

Blessed are those who mourn, for they will be comforted.

—Matthew 5:4 (NIV)

MEMORIES

What are some songs, scents, places, etc. that elicit a distinct memory in you? Why do you think that memory is so powerful to you?

2

HANDLING WHAT WE GET

Shortly after Amy's passing, our family took a second blow from cancer. My mom was diagnosed with kidney cancer. Luckily, it was located on the top of her kidney, and she was able to have it surgically removed. She didn't need chemo or radiation. However, just a few short years later, she was diagnosed with colon cancer. All the lingo and jargon that were once foreign to us were becoming second nature. We knew what to expect and when to worry. Mom was declared cancer-free only to have it return. Again, my faith in God was wavering. Why us again? Haven't we paid our dues? People would say God only gives us what we can handle. Well, God had a lot more faith in us than I did. I wanted someone else to have to handle it. Selfishly, I wondered, Why can't it be someone else's family?

Have you ever told someone, "God doesn't give us more than we can handle?" Do you know where that comes from? I have never cared for that saying, as I felt like people were trivializing what someone was going through. *Oh, you'll be fine, you can handle it, it's not that big a deal, or God wouldn't have given it to you.* Likewise, it makes it sound like the bad things in our lives come from God. Actually, this saying is a twist of scripture. In 1 Corinthians 10:13, it says, "No temptation has overtaken you except what is common to mankind. And God is faithful; he will not let you be tempted beyond what you can bear. But when you are tempted, he will also provide a way out so that you can endure it."

As you can see, this scripture is about temptation and sin. It is telling us that God will not put us in situations where temptation to do wrong is irresistible but will always make a way for us to escape. It's saying we are responsible for our own choices or temptations and reminds us that we are capable of not doing the things we should not be doing. This has nothing to do with God handing us burdens and sorrows because we are strong. What we should remember is that God gives us the *tools* so we can handle whatever life throws at us. It's not God choosing to put bad things in our life.

At the end of 2015, Mom took a bad turn. In January of 2016, the decision was made to place her in hospice. Although she wanted to go home, it wasn't feasible. Her body organs were shutting down, and taking her home wasn't going to be possible in the time frame we had to work with. She ended up in the hospice unit at the hospital. We put out a call to her family and friends that she was near the end, and if they wanted to say their goodbyes, they should come the following day. So many people came that we lost count. It was a steady stream the entire day.

After everyone had left, Mom was moved up to the hospice floor. Her one request was to be able to see her kitty one last time. While mom was sick, her cat, Mace, was often brought up. She was overly worried about who would take Mace when she died. She kept asking my youngest brother, Jordan, to take him. Jordan would pacify her and say yes. Then, he would turn to us and say, "I'm not taking that cat!" Well, after pulling some strings with the hospice nurses, they told us we could bring Mace for a visit.

I should let you know that Jordan was not a cat person. However, he was chosen to go get the cat and bring it to the hospital. Now, if you aren't a cat person, you probably don't know the hideous, loud I'm-about-to-die cry that comes from many cats when they are in a vehicle. Jordan wasn't aware of that, but he learned really quick on the thirty-minute ride to the hospital!

My best friend, Gretel, had come to visit me, and we were sitting on the main floor of the hospital near the elevators when we heard it. Long before we could see Jordan, we could hear Mace. He was mad, whining as loud as he could, freaking out in his carrier because of the car ride and now the new smells of a hospital. Jordan had thrown a towel over the cage, so bystanders could hear it but had no idea what Jordan was carrying! Mace continued to carry on in the elevator. We were starting to rethink our decision to bring the cat to see her. However, when the doors to the elevator opened and we stepped onto the hospice floor, Mace became silent. He never made another peep. I got him out of the carrier and handed him to Mom. Mace is not an overly loving cat, so holding him wasn't always what Mace was willing to let you do. But Mace went to Mom and laid in her hospital bed with her. She talked to him and petted him until she eventually said it was enough and to take him. We put him back in his carrier, and he continued to remain quiet until Jordan eventually took him home.

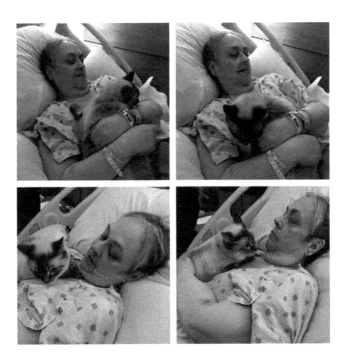

Just a month after Christmas, January 26, 2016, my mom passed away at the age of sixty-three. My grandma's birthday (Mom's mom) was January 26, and Gram was so worried Mom would die on her birthday, and she did. I was there when she took her last breath. While I am glad I was able to be there when she died, it is an image I have never forgotten.

I had never seen a person take their last breath. I'm not sure what I expected, but it didn't happen any way close to what I thought would happen. Shortly before passing, Mom was raising her arms into the air like she was reaching for something. Then, she put them back down and her breath slowed. After a couple minutes, her breaths slowed to the point of only one or two a minute. Then, her chest rose and fell one more time, and that was the end—very peaceful.

At this point, I was done. I was mad at God. We had prayed. Our church had prayed. Our entire community of friends and family had prayed, yet our prayers weren't answered. Again, I wondered, *What did we do wrong to be punished like this?*

By the way, Jordan caved in and took Mace to live with him just as Mom had asked. He still has Mace, who lives daily to irritate and torment Jordan, much to my Mom's delight I'm sure!

But ask the animals, and they will teach you, or the birds in the sky, and they will tell you; or speak to the earth, and it will teach you, or let the fish in the sea inform you, Which of all these does not know that the hand of the Lᴏʀᴅ has done this? In his hand is the life of every creature and the breath of all mankind.

—Job 12:7–10 (NIV)

Take this time to reflect on a very difficult time in your life. Then, go back through and circle the tools God gave you to survive that difficult time. Did he bring new people into your life? Did a new job opportunity come from it? Did you find a way to pay the debts you thought you'd never get repaid?

3

TREASURES

Just prior to my mom's passing, we learned of cancer yet again, rearing its ugly head. This time, it was my thirty-one-year-old cousin, Laura. Right around Christmastime, she was diagnosed with breast cancer. Laura, her sister Kristi, and I share a special bond. We are more like sisters than cousins. I have always treasured the closeness I feel to these two. We grew up in the same area, and we attended the same church while growing up. We were even in a singing group together called Sisters with Christian Soul. Laura and I also played the organ and piano for our church. While we were close growing up, we became closer as adults. We were always finding ways to get together whether it be to work out, play games, or just going out to eat.

Pictured: me (right), Laura (middle), Kristi (right), and Lila Mae (three weeks old). This picture was taken shortly after Laura's diagnosis.

Shortly after the passing of Amy, Jeremy decided to participate in a cancer fundraising biking event that was held each year in our community. In 2015, Laura had decided to participate. Ironically, the path the bikes take comes directly past the farm that our family grew up on. Each year, we meet at my Aunt Pat's house to cheer on the thousands of riders who are riding to end cancer. Little did Laura know, the hospital she was fundraising for in August would soon be the hospital tasked with saving her life just a few short months later.

Laura spent a year battling through surgery, chemo, and radiation. By the end of 2016, she was declared in remission, but not without another cousin, Andrea, also being diagnosed with lymphoma that same summer. Andrea is younger than Laura. Both cousins were able to end 2016 with their health, and our family was finally cancer-free. This still didn't help, though. I still wanted to know why. Why did we have to keep going through this? Why couldn't we catch a break? I stopped going to church during this time. I was mad at God and questioning if he really existed. What was happening to all our prayers? Why were they being ignored? What were we doing wrong?

In the summer of 2019, it started all over again. Yet another cousin, Amy, was diagnosed with breast cancer. Technically, she is my dad's cousin, but she is the same age as me. Around this same time, we found out that Laura's breast cancer was back and back with a vengeance. It had metastasized to her bones and brain. It affected her vision and landed her back in the hospital and back on treatments. After ten years of cancer in our family, we knew what this meant. She did her best to continue battling this beast, which had now entered her brain and her hip among other places. I had always been in awe of her strength and poise during her battle.

In June of 2021, Laura chose to stop chemo. It was making her sick all the time and was not doing anything other than slowing down the spread of cancer. The cancer was still consuming her body. Hospice was called in, and Laura passed peacefully from this earth on June 5, 2021, at the age of thirty-seven.

Despite her prognosis, Laura was always upbeat and positive, but toward the end, even she was starting to question it. Lots of the family began questioning it. "How many times do we have to deal with this? Why us?"

Pictured: Kristi (left), me (middle), Laura (right), taken on July 4, 2016, six months into Laura's breast cancer treatments

For where your treasure is, there your heart will also be.

—Luke 12:34 (NIV)

Think about this verse: "For where your treasure is, there your heart will also be." So often we take our treasures for granted. Use this space to list everything you treasure. (And yes, it's fine to have chocolate on the list!) Be creative!

4

ROY CLYDE!

y grandpa's name was Roy Clyde (my mom's dad). I called him Pops. Roy Clyde was what my gram called him when he was being ornery or was cussing! He was only a cusser when something wasn't working right. I'm pretty sure his favorite and most used line was "What in the Sam Hell?" to which Gram would always fire back from the other room, "Roy Clyde!" Then he would just laugh and move on. I think sometimes he did it just to get a rise out of her.

My grandparents were married for sixty-eight years! You read that right, sixty-eight years! They were married for twenty-two years longer than I have even yet been alive.

Pops and Gram lived independently up until a year before they died. That's not to say they didn't have occasions where their ability to stay alone was questioned, for example, the time my Gram fell when going out to get the mail. She hollered and hollered for Pops, but he couldn't hear you if you were in the same room, let alone her being outside. Eventually, he realized she was missing and went looking for her. Unfortunately, Pops couldn't get her up, so being the innovative and creative thinking man he was, he had an idea of how to best get her up. I'm sure you are thinking, *Oh, he called for someone to come help her*, and that would be logical thinking. I didn't say logical; I said innovative and creative. Nope, Pops didn't call anyone. He went and got the tractor with a backhoe/scoop and lifted her up that way! I only wish we could've had a video. So many things could've gone wrong with this plan, but it didn't. He got her up without inconveniencing anyone else and made for a good laugh after we got over the horror of the what ifs!

Pops was not one to inconvenience others. If he could do it himself, he would, sometimes even when he shouldn't have. Pops had a shop where he worked on tractors, farming equipment, etc. and was a place he could often be found. One day, he was working on a tractor, and somehow it came loose/out of gear, knocked him down, and ran over him. Yes, I said ran over him. He was by himself, so he did the only logical thing to do in his mind. He got up, walked down the hill to where the tractor had rolled, drove it back up to the shop. Then, he got in his truck and drove back to the house where Gram was (a half mile or so away) and went in the house and told her he thought "maybe she ought to run him up to the hospital to get checked over." This would be one of those "*Roy Clyde*" moments when he told her why he wanted to get checked out. Pops was instantly transferred to the trauma unit at Grant hospital where it was determined he had broken every single rib. Yes, Pops, you needed to get checked out!

Despite his occasional cussing, my grandfather was a godly man. He went to church every Sunday and went to Bible studies on Wednesday nights. He taught a Sunday school class and was an elder in the church. My gram was also a Sunday school teacher for many years and played the piano for the church Many times, I would walk into my grandparents' home, and Pops would be sitting at his desk, reading from the Bible. I have no doubt God was sitting beside him on the tractor, guiding him to "gently" get Gram up off the ground and that God was with him when that tractor ran over him.

In late 2017, Pops and Gram were headed in town to go to their normal routine lunch or dinner at Southside restaurant when Pops fell off the porch. He wasn't as lucky this time and ended up with a broken hip. Pops never returned home after that. He spent the rest of his days in a nursing facility with my Gram faithfully visiting him every day. Pops passed in May of 2018. Gram followed him home to the Lord just six months later, dying peacefully in her sleep.

Despite many hardships in their life, one of the hardest things my Pops and Gram had to do was bury a child. My Gram would have done anything in the world to help save my mom's life. In fact, she even went so far as to ask me if I knew any of "those people who grow or sell marijuana" and if not, did I "know somewhere we could go buy some!" Instead of that being followed by "*Roy Clyde*," it was me saying "Gram!" She said she was old and willing to spare any expense, even if it meant going to jail for buying weed, to save my mom. Needless to say, I didn't know "any of those people," and Gram decided it was probably best we didn't go that route anyway. But that goes to show the love someone can have for someone else. She was willing to do anything, including going to jail, to help my mom.

My grandparents were two peas in a pod. It's not surprising that they went to their final resting place within six months of each other. Sixty-eight years is a long time to spend with someone, and imagine the loneliness that each of them felt, being away from each other during that last year. I miss my grandparents like crazy. They taught me so much in terms of morals and work ethic as well as being role models in relationships. We all need a love like theirs—one that surpasses time and continues despite squabbles and disagreements. Pops never gave up on Gram, and in turn, she never gave up on him even though she wanted to thump him upside the head sometimes! "Husbands, love your wives, just as Christ loved the church and gave himself up for her" (Ephesians 5:25).

And now these three remain: faith, hope, and
love. But the greatest of these is love.

—1 Corinthians 13:13 (NIV)

Negotiations

My grandparents' marriage was able to survive sixty-eight years because of give-and-take as well as a whole lot of patience and forgiveness and negotiation. What are your non-negotiables in a relationship? Why are they nonnegotiable? Are any of your non-negotiables something that has ended a relationship? Looking back, should you have negotiated better, or was it a good choice?

5

HERE IT COMES

When I developed a rash in October of 2019, my first thoughts went to my cousin Laura and how that had been one of her body's warning signs. She had had a clear mammogram just months before, so she did not immediately think the rash was a sign of concern. My rash was about an inch and a half by about half an inch and was on the underside of my left breast, close to where the heart is located. It was basically bright red and itchy. That was about it, no bumps, no peeling, just redness. I had no other symptoms that would tell me something was wrong.

I tried some over-the-counter remedies, but the rash just wasn't going away. Honestly, I thought it was a rash from boob sweat. Women, you know what I'm talking about! I've been a horrible sweater since having a hysterectomy in 2015. I would sweat when it was negative ten degrees outside. So I waited for about two weeks before my intuition said I had to get it checked. Something just didn't seem right.

As I wasn't scheduled to have a mammogram until January, I contacted my family doctor and asked if she could schedule it early. I did not mention the rash or why I had wanted to do this early. I wanted to see if anything was found before I mentioned the rash, especially if it turned out it was just a rash from boob sweat. I had my initial mammogram on Monday, October 21. Oddly enough, the rash disappeared that day. It was just gone, no redness, nothing. I went ahead with the mammogram with the thought that the rash was actually nothing since it had finally gone away. I'd have my mammogram done for the year and go on with my life.

Unfortunately, the results came back that I needed additional imaging. There was one spot against the chest wall that they wanted better imaging of. It showed up in one picture but not in any of the others. I had a diagnostic mammogram on Friday, October 25. The results came back with a possible malignancy in the left side. This was exactly where the rash had been. Now I was becoming concerned. They scheduled a biopsy for Thursday, October 31. During my prebiopsy questioning, I finally mentioned the rash. I told her where it had been and how it was the reason I had come in to begin with. She looked but saw nothing on the skin. I told her it had basically disappeared once I came in for the initial mammogram.

I met with the doctor who would be doing the biopsy. He told me that he wasn't sure if there was anything to biopsy as the spot showed up on the initial mammogram on one picture but was not present on the second images. He said he wanted to do additional imaging prior to trying the biopsy. If it still couldn't be seen, he was going to cancel the biopsy. He said it was possible it was a shadow or even remnants from lotion or body wash that left a shadow. I headed back with the two technicians. I have to give those ladies credit; they worked their butts off to find the spot. At one point, I'm pretty sure I was standing on one foot, with one arm up and one arm behind my back with my head tipped backwards. One of the techs was underneath me holding my skin taut while the image was taken. It was very uncomfortable, but they found the spot!

We could now move on to the biopsy. Because of the location of the suspicious spot, the biopsy ended up taking three hours. If you've never had a breast biopsy before, it is an interesting process. You are placed facedown on a table that has a hole where your breast is dropped down in. Your table is then lifted up toward the ceiling, and they work on you from under the table. Imagine a mechanic putting your car on a lift so they can see under your car. That's exactly what it is like! I can't really say it is a painful procedure although I do have a very high pain tolerance. It's more uncomfortable than anything. Plus all you can really see is the ceiling, so it's pretty boring.

When I left, they told me it would be three to five days before I got any results and that would not include the weekend. Less than twenty-four hours later, while unloading groceries in the Kroger parking lot, my doctor's office called. I knew before I even answered the phone. "Hi, Jill. We have the results of your biopsy. We need you to come in as soon as possible, and we need you to bring someone with you." Again, I was not new to this. I knew it was cancer.

But I will restore you to health and heal your wounds.

—Jeremiah 30:17 (NIV)

Take this time to write down what yearly appointments you (or your spouse) have been neglecting. *Call your doctor and get them done!*

Mammogram?
Colonoscopy?
Yearly pap?
Cholesterol screening?
Diabetes screening?
Prostate exam?
Yearly physical?

Early detection saves lives.

6

OVERCOMER

The following Monday, I went with my husband, Kevin, to the doctor's office. I should also mention that Kevin and I had just been married for three months at this point. We got married on my grandparents' anniversary! I figured it was a good date for them since they made it sixty-eight years. Hopefully, it would be a good date for us as well.

The doctor said the words no one wanted to hear: "You have breast cancer." I had come in prepared, prepared in knowledge already of what I had because I looked it up on my online health portal. This was another thing we unfortunately had learned to use religiously through all the cancers in our family. Unbeknownst to my doctor, I also came with vast knowledge in the cancer world. She mentioned that I seemed to handle the news well. Unfortunately, cancer diagnosis was becoming commonplace in our family. I didn't cry in the office or even on the way home. Why? Because I was mad. Furious would be a better word. Why was this happening? Why me? Why did God allow this to happen to me? I had been back in church for two years at this point. I had just gotten married three months prior to this to a Christian man. My husband and I attended church every Sunday with my stepdaughters Ava and Emma. I had just taken a position as one of the Children's Ministry coordinators. Now my faith was being tested yet again.

By Thursday of the same week, I was transferred to a different hospital system (my request). I had an appointment with the same surgeon my cousin, Laura, had started with. At that point, the blur began. I had a breast MRI, met with my nurse navigator, had genetic testing, was fitted for surgical bras, met with a cancer counselor, met with a breast reconstruction surgeon, and finally went through pre-surgical testing all within a ten-day period. I also worked full time during all this, only missing two days of work. I wanted to keep my mind busy. My work family was beyond awesome during this time. I couldn't ask for more understanding from my coworkers.

I had a bilateral (double) mastectomy on Wednesday, December 11, 2019. I was given a choice of a single or double mastectomy. Kevin and I were in agreement that I should have a double. With the amount of cancer in my family history, why take the risk? Turns out we made the right choice. The pathology report showed all kinds of abnormalities and calcifications in the right breast that easily could've turned to cancer. Likewise, there was more cancer present than had been visible on the mammograms.

My husband, Kevin, and stepdaughters Ava and Emma in 2018

Oddly enough, during the forty-one days from diagnosis to surgery, I found myself changing. I was so bitter in the beginning. So many thoughts were going through me. Would I need chemo?

Would I need a mastectomy? Was I going to be bald? How were we going to pay for this? Would my husband leave me? He surely didn't sign up to have a wife who would be going through a major medical issue three months after getting married. Would having a mastectomy leave me deformed? I already had a horrible self-image; this wasn't going to help that.

But I discovered I was praying more often. I wasn't as angry at God anymore. My heart was softening. I wasn't really sure why. However, there was something I was discovering. There were an awful lot of people who cared for me. I was receiving gifts and well-wishes from people I hadn't seen in years. Organizations and churches I didn't even attend were helping me out. My faith in humanity was taking a huge upward swing.

When I was asked what radio station I wanted on during my hour and a half MRI, I requested a worship station. I lay there in that small tube, on my stomach, in the superman position (arms straight up on the sides of my head with elbows on my ears) for an hour and a half and prayed. I listened to the words of the songs and thought about how they fit in my life. I have no doubt God picked those songs that were played because they spoke directly to my situation. The very first song that was played was "Overcomer" sung by Mandisa. If you've never heard the song, I encourage you to listen to it.

I don't know why. I don't know how, but finally, I was at peace. I was no longer praying for the cancer to go away as I knew that was more of asking for a miracle. I was no longer praying and asking, "Why me?" As the song said, I was staying in this fight until it was over. There was no giving up. There was no going under. God had me, and he knew exactly what he was doing. Now my prayers have changed to "how can I use what I am going through to help others?" I finally realized lying in that uncomfortable loud tube, on my stomach, with my head pressed downward in a pillow, and my arms out like superman, that there was a reason God put me in this position… and I was finally at peace with it.

Peace I leave with you; my peace I give you. I do
not give to you as the world gives. Do not let your
hearts be troubled and do not be afraid.

—John 14:27 (NIV)

Music has always been a very big part of my life. Specific songs can bring back memories and tug at your heart like nothing else can do. Make a list of songs that have meaning to you. Why are they so special to you?

7

TELLING

As a cancer survivor, I have to say that, in my case, the most difficult part of the journey wasn't the diagnosis, the pain of the biopsy or the MRI, and not even the pain of the mastectomy. The hardest part of all was telling people. Since I had not told many people about the rash or the screenings, most people had no clue that anything could be wrong with me. I wasn't outwardly sick. In fact, had it not been for the rash, I never would've suspected I had cancer growing in my body.

I don't think telling people I had cancer was the part that was hard; it was watching their reaction to the news. The ones I told on the phone were by far easier than the face-to-face ones. I am not a person who wants people feeling sorry for me. I'm not big on sharing emotions either. So watching people's faces be in shock and then sink when they heard the news was hard for me. I knew they were taking pity on me, and I didn't want pity. I also knew many were thinking of my mother who had died of cancer just three years prior. In some cases, I simply asked someone I had told to tell someone else for me. I think when someone tells you they have cancer, it's very awkward because what do you say? I'm sorry? Oh no? Um…what do you say?

Honestly though, of all the people I told, one group was the absolute worst. That was my students. I've been a teacher for twenty-one years. More than once I've had to tell my students things that were difficult. But standing in front of three separate classes of twenty-six ten- and eleven-year-olds and saying "your teacher has cancer" is not an easy thing to do. It's especially hard when you've barely had time to process it yourself. First of all, they were blindsided just as everyone else was. Sure, they knew I had missed two days of school, but teachers miss school all the time. Secondly, they are fifth graders. They all have had different interactions with cancer in their lifetime. It was not hard at all to pick out the students who knew someone who died from cancer, as they were tearing up and avoiding eye contact. I did not go into much detail with them. I mean, do fifth graders want to hear their teacher talk about breasts? I simply said I needed to tell them that I was going to be leaving for a while and they would be having a substitute. I said I was leaving because they had found cancer in my body and I needed to have it surgically removed. I assured them that I would be back by the end of January and that I would make sure their other teachers kept them up to date on my progress. I specifically told them on a Friday at the end of their class because I wanted them to have the weekend to process the news. Likewise, I also emailed each of their parents and told them what I had told their children that day. The students did not say much to me other than a couple asking if I was sure I was going to be okay. I knew they were in shock, and this was something many of them had never dealt with before. At the same time, I go back to what I said before, what do you say to someone who just told you they have cancer?

I can't even describe the outpouring that came from my students' parents that weekend. I teach in a very diverse district. We have many different languages and many different religions, but one thing was clear—they all believed in the power of prayer and healing. Here are some excerpts of just a few of the many letters I received:

Dear ma'am,

I am sorry to hear about your health condition. Hope your health will be good after surgery. God gives you the strength to fight against that disease. And I thank you for letting us (parents) know about that.

Again, I pray for your speedy recovery.

You are in our thoughts and prayers. As the daughter of a cancer survivor, I know that the power of prayer (whatever type of prayer that is for everyone) is amazing! Sending good vibes.

I'm so sorry to hear of your diagnosis. I am a two-year cancer survivor, so I know how you are feeling right now. I want you to know that I will keep you in my thoughts and prayers.

Do everything the doctors tell you and keep on the regiment they put you on! I will be rooting for you! Please don't stress through the holidays—I know that's easier said than done. But enjoy the time with family and worry after!

God bless.

I just wanted to tell you that our thoughts and prayers are with you during this time. I wish you the best of luck with surgery and recovery. Your health matters, so don't worry about your students not being taken care of. I'm sure your short-term sub and your team of teachers will be able to make sure everything is in order. I hope you have a wonderful Thanksgiving and a restful, happy holidays.

My prayers will be with you all the way through. God will carry you through, just remember, and in those difficult times he is really carrying you. Hang in there and if there's anything I can do to help you through this difficult time, please do not hesitate to ask. If you would like a meal or just a helping hand somewhere, please I will be very happy to assist you.

While I know their children well, many of these parents I do not know well, some I have never even met. So to receive the outpouring of prayer and hope I received was heartwarming. The following week, I received numerous gifts. One was a prayer blanket that one of the students' mom had crocheted for me.

That week, the students started opening up too. I was getting a lot of hugs and a lot of drawings and cards. The students were full of questions that fifth graders would logically have. Who is going to be our sub? Do you have to stay at the hospital the whole time? Will you be able to walk? (Remember, they didn't know what kind of cancer I had.) Will you lose your hair? Slowly word spread to students who were not in any of my classes, students I didn't even know would walk up to me and say, "I'm sorry to hear you have cancer, Mrs. Dorman." or "I hope your surgery goes okay, Mrs. Dorman." One thing about working with kids, they can drive you absolutely batty and, the next minute, have your heart swelling in pride of their maturity and sincere concern for their teacher.

A 3D card from one of my students

When I was thinking about the outpouring from my students' parents, I was thinking about people in other professions. I didn't have to do it, but I shared the personal details of my health with seventy-five sets of students and their parents. Most people would only need to tell their boss and a couple coworkers. Teaching is an odd profession. Many times, we spend more time with the students than their parents do on a daily basis. Those students become our family. We think about them even when we aren't at work. And now the tables were turned. The students and their parents were having conversations and praying for me. If there is one thing I've learned about cancer, you can never have too many people praying for you, and I had an army.

Therefore confess your sins to each other, and pray
for each other so that you may be healed. The prayer
of a righteous person is powerful and effective.

—James 5:16 (NIV)

Do you have a favorite teacher from your childhood? Mine would be my junior high reading teacher, Miss Dunlap. I had her class right after lunch, and she read aloud to us every day. She chose the best books, and I loved listening to her read. She also didn't take any guff off the many hooligans who were in my classes (We were always told we were the worst class to come through the school system). It was my favorite part of the day. Who was your favorite teacher or school staff member? What made them so special to you?

8

SECOND FAMILY

Speaking of armies, my cancer journey brought out many. Not even two years prior to my diagnosis, I made several huge life changes. After almost twenty years teaching in the same small school district, I made a change. I took a leap of faith and interviewed to be a gifted teacher in the district ten minutes from my house. I did not know anyone who worked in the district. I almost didn't even go to the interview because of this. How could I go from being one of the teachers with the most seniority to the new teacher? How do I leave teaching with my best friend and go somewhere I know no one?

I'm not overly outgoing and am very quiet in situations where I don't know many people, so this was definitely stepping out of the box for me. I knew I needed this life change, so I went for it. Within five minutes of starting the interview, I knew these people interviewing me were genuine. I felt comfortable with them, and the overall school had a homey feel. I accepted the position, and it was one of the best decisions I've ever made in my career.

Little did I know that fifteen months after starting there, these people who were once strangers to me would be some of my biggest cheerleaders. Research shows that if you and your coworkers feel like a community and have great rapport with one another, the more likely it is that you'll feel psychologically and physically healthy at work.

When word about my cancer spread, my coworkers came out in full force to support me. I was asked constantly how they could help, what they could do, and what would be the most helpful for me? Now, my coworkers at North Elementary were stellar to begin with. It's a staff like I've never been a part of before. You could go to anyone in that building and they would do anything they could to help you regardless if you had cancer or not. We worked in teams at that time, and I knew that my team of Heather Landgraver, Angie Hemmert, and Nick Horton would keep my classes going and take care of anything needed at the school. The day I left for extended leave for surgery, I received a huge outpouring of gifts, gift cards, a cake, flowers, and more to send me off with a smile. For people I barely knew just a year before, I felt like I was leaving my family behind that day, especially my "school neighbors" Denise Nugent and Cheryl Harger.

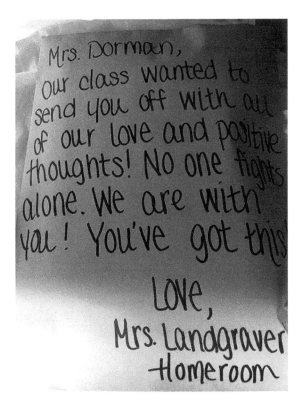

When I got home from surgery, I had a visit from three of them and texts or phone calls from nearly all the rest. They brought more gifts and lots of smiles and (gentle) hugs. Knowing these coworkers were taking care of anything the substitutes in my classroom needed was a huge help to me. Speaking of substitutes, my long-term sub, Cara Huizinga, was a rock star. Anyone who works in education knows that the weeks before Christmas break are long, tiring, and crazy. Cara stepped in and took over my class during that crazy time. I knew she would take care of everything. I was very blessed to have such wonderful coworkers at that time. Coworkers can make or break your job.

Have you ever had a job that you simply dreaded going to? You didn't like the people who worked with you. You didn't like your boss. If you think about that same job, would you have liked the actual job if the other (annoying) people weren't there? I've been in this situation, and while I enjoyed my job, I did not enjoy the other people who were at my job. This caused stress, anxiety, and overwhelming feelings. Why do people have that much effect on us? Maybe the better question is why do we let people have that much effect on us?

Situations like this remind me of the story of Daniel and the lion's den. Daniel had two "coworkers" who were jealous that the king put Daniel in charge of the kingdom. They decided to try to find a past scandal or skeleton in his closet.

Have you ever had that happen to you? Unfortunately, I have. Sometimes people cannot handle that some people want to do well at their job and are willing to put in the extra work to succeed. Instead of rooting those people on, some people ridicule them and call them "pets" of the leader or boss. They call you a suck up and make you feel badly for wanting to do your best.

Back to Daniel, these two men were unable to find anything to get him on, so they convinced the king to sign a decree that anyone who prayed to God would be thrown in the lion's den. They then snuck to his house and caught him praying. The king had no choice but to throw him into the lion's den. The two men were happy they had succeeded in destroying Daniel. But little did they know, God was protecting Daniel from those lions. The next morning, Daniel was removed from the den with not even a scratch on him. The two men were then thrown in the den and the lions were not as nice to them. What was the difference? Daniel was being protected by the God he prayed to. The other two did not pray to God and thus were not protected.

What did Daniel do when his coworkers were out to get him? He showed up to work anyway. He continued to do his job anyway. Not only did he continue to work, he continued to do it well. But he didn't have to do this alone. He prayed to God for help, and God took care of Daniel. So what should we do in cases where we have coworkers we struggle to find the good in? Show up for work anyway. Continue to do your job anyway. But you need to do more than that. You need to pray for those coworkers. Pray for them and think of a way to thank God for your current circumstance. Be like Daniel.

But as for you, be strong and do not give up,
for your work will be rewarded.

—2 Chronicles 15:7 (NIV)

Coworkers often become our second family. Sometimes we are with them for more hours out of the day than our own families. Make a list of your current and past coworkers who made work more fun. Think back to every job you have had. Put a star by those you are still in contact with. If you don't have stars next to all of them, I encourage you to contact them and remind them how much they mean/meant to you.

9

THE HAND-HOLDER

Only forty-one days passed between the biopsy and the mastectomy. While my nurse navigator was wonderful, my doctors were super thorough, and the nurses gave me printed copies of directions. There was still a lot I do not think I fully absorbed during all those visits and tests. I do remember the nurse navigator talking to me about the sentinel node injection. She warned me about how painful it would seem and what to expect afterwards, but honestly, I did not recall most of what she told me.

In most breast cancer cases, doctors need to take a couple lymph nodes to make sure cancer hasn't spread there. This involves injecting a dye known as a tracer, which helps light up the sentinel nodes to help the surgeons with removal. As if you don't have enough foreign things going on in your body, this injection also can cause your urine to be blue!

My sentinel node injection was scheduled the morning of my mastectomy. As I said, I remembered them saying it would be painful, but that's about all I remembered. I had already had a biopsy where they dug around with a needle for three hours, so I didn't think this would be much more than that. I also have a very high pain tolerance, so I wasn't worried.

The guy doing the injection came to get me and off we went to radiology. He was cracking jokes and had me laughing. He told me he was going to go grab my records and he would be right back. He jokingly said, "I promise not to leave you down here and disappear." He no sooner left the room than a crazy noise went off, lights started blinking, and the door to the room went shut on its own! I'm not one to scare easily, but I didn't know what the heck was going on. I heard voices outside the door and saw the door handle rattle like someone was trying to get it, but no one came in. I was just about to the point of starting to freak out when the noise stopped, and the guy opened the door. He started apologizing right away. He said the fire alarm had gone off unexpectedly, which caused the magnets holding the doors open to release their magnetism. The door shut, and he had not unlocked the door that morning, so I was locked in the room while he went to get a key!

Once the craziness of that was over and my heart rate came back down, he said, "I'm going to go get the hand-holder and we will be ready to start." I thought maybe I heard him wrong. Why would I need a hand-holder? If I needed that, they should've let my husband come back with me. He returned with a nice little older lady who came right up to my bed and took my hand. She told me she has held the hands of thousands of women when they have done this and to not be afraid to squeeze her hand because no one has broken it yet. Now, I was starting to wonder what exactly this test was going to be like. So I asked, which was a bad idea. Sometimes it's better to just let them do the procedure so you don't know what's coming. He told me that he would be injecting a needle into my nipple that would release the dye needed to light up the nodes. Already that made me squeamish. Then, he proceeds to tell me that it will feel like one thousand bees stinging me all at the same time, but that the pain would only last for a couple minutes. He then asked if I was ready. Um...how could anyone be ready after that? It was right then that a Bible verse popped into my head, Proverbs 21:31. Do your best, prepare for the worst, then trust God to bring victory. The best I could do is lay there and pray, and that's exactly what I did.

The hand-holder lady grabbed my hand; the other one was tied down because it had the IV meds and stuff in it. On the count of three, he started. Did it hurt? Hurt is an understatement. He was right about the one thousand bees stinging you over and over and over in a very tender part of your body. I squeezed that poor lady's hand like there was no tomorrow. Just when I felt like I needed to scream, it stopped. Just like that. Over.

I would love to see my heart rate monitoring from my time in the radiology appointment—calm, to freaked out, to calm, to freaked out, to major pain, to calm, all in the course of about twenty minutes!

I was wheeled back to my room, feeling rather radioactive but, other than that, back to normal. I couldn't help but wonder if my reaction to the injection would have been different if I had not asked him what to expect. In one regard, by asking him I knew it would be over in a matter of minutes. On the other hand, I had visions of bees stinging me before he even started, so did it feel like bees because that's what I was told to feel or because it really did feel like that.

So often in life, we are swayed by the opinions and beliefs of others. Social media and the news are prime examples of this. But have you ever stopped to think about how much you influence others without even trying to or even meaning to? One day, my husband went and got doughnuts and coffee from a local chain restaurant. When he took a drink of the coffee, he said, "Ugh, that tastes like dirty water." Emma, my stepdaughter, instantly decided hers tasted like dirty water and refused to even try it. She eventually did but immediately made a sour face and said it tasted like dirty water—the exact same words his father had said. Had he not said that, maybe she would have drunk the coffee and maybe she would not have. But she was influenced by his taste of the coffee enough to believe it wasn't worth her even trying it.

Every word we speak or action we take in life matters. People are always watching us and are sometimes making decisions based on what they see us do. If kids see a parent cursing and screaming at the other parent, they are going to think it's okay for them to do the same. If someone hears you playing music that involves cussing, sex, and drugs, they will think those songs are okay too. Are you setting a good example and influence for others? Or do you need to work on the way you influence others?

Imitate God in everything you do, because you are his dear
children. Live a life filled with love following the example of
Christ. He loved us and offered himself as a sacrifice to us.

—Ephesians 5:1–2 (NLT)

Role Models

Everyone has had a role model at some point in their life. Maybe it was a relative, maybe a teacher, or maybe someone you met at work or school. How did that person influence your life? How is your life better because of that person? Have you told them what a difference they made in your life? If not, why haven't you?

10

TRUST THE PROCESS

I have never done well with anesthesia. I wake up from surgery, and I vomit for what seems like eternity. This surgery was no different and maybe even worse because I was under for more than eight hours. Waking up in the recovery room, the first thing I noticed was how hot I was. I was sweating like crazy. I tried to move the blanket off of me, but it felt like it weighed a thousand pounds. The second thing I noticed while trying to move that blanket was that my sternum felt like it had been ripped in two. If I laid really still, it did not hurt. But any movement made it feel like my breastbone was splitting in half again. That feeling actually lasted for close to a week. It subsided, but the pain was always there for a good month or two. I later discovered the reason I couldn't move the blanket was because I wasn't actually gripping the blanket. My fingertips were numb, and I didn't realize it. So while I thought I was grabbing the blanket and thought I was pushing the numbers on the remote, I wasn't because I couldn't feel them. I had trouble gripping things for a long time after surgery.

While the first twelve hours after surgery were miserable due to nausea from the anesthesia, as soon as that was out of my system, I was a new person. Within a two-hour time period, I went from not being able to sit up without vomiting to eating a full breakfast, walking a lap around the hallway, making it to the bathroom on my own, and sitting in the chair to talk to my cousins (the ones I mentioned in an earlier chapter). Both doctors came in and found that since I'd improved so quickly, I was being given the okay to be dismissed! I was home less than twenty-four hours after I came out of surgery. I would have been sent home sooner had I not vomited so long. Fun Fact: A mastectomy is considered outpatient surgery! Can you believe that?

With a double mastectomy and reconstruction at the same time, I was told I would need to be off work for six to eight weeks. Honestly, the first two weeks were a blur. I slept a lot and watched a lot of TV shows. My best friend, Gretel Lloyd, came over and helped me wash my hair in the kitchen sink a few days after I got home. On day 4, I decided to attempt the shower. I came home with four drains in, so in order to take a shower, I needed to hold those up. In the blur of the weeks leading up to surgery, I think I missed the memo that getting a lanyard is good to help with drains. Well, we didn't have a lanyard handy, but Kevin had an old belt. So, we hung his belt around my neck, strapped the drains to that, and I made my way to the shower. I should've gone directly to the shower, but I caught a glimpse of myself on the way to the bathroom and decided to do a closer inspection. That's when the real tears came, not the physical pain tears but the emotional tears. Nothing on earth can prepare you to look in that mirror the first time and see yourself flat-chested. They were gone. I looked like a man. I knew in my mind that one day with the reconstruction, they would fill back out, but in that moment, nothing could console me from that loss. I had many people tell me not to have reconstruction, just go flat, why hassle with it. It's because it's my body, and part of my body was taken away forever, that's why. It's because it's my body, and the part that makes me feminine was gone, that's why. I managed to make my way to the shower, and Kevin helped me to reinsert myself into the surgical bra and binding that was needed. I needed a nap after all that, but that shower felt so good!

At the one-week mark, I mastered the shower on my own. Laura and Kristi tag teamed to get me to the doctor that day as well. I stopped taking pain pills after three days of being home. I was still taking ibuprofen, but oddly enough, I wasn't in pain except for the sternum and that was only when I was getting up and down. Uncomfortable, oh my gosh, yes, but pain, not at all. When the nurse came to get me in the waiting room, she told me I looked excellent for only a week out.

This was me one week out from surgery. I showered
and did my hair myself for the first time.

Fast forward four weeks, one month out from a double mastectomy with reconstruction. I went for my weekly doctor check, and he cleared me to return to work! At four weeks! He said I was a model patient, and when he left the room, he turned back around at the door and said, "I'm so proud of you for trusting the process."

Those were words I needed to hear. You see, I'm a very independent person. I don't like to ask for help...ever. When I woke up from surgery and I couldn't move my arms enough to lift a spoon close enough to my mouth to eat ice chips, when I couldn't get to the bathroom without someone helping me, when I got home and it took me an hour and a half just to take a shower and get dressed (with Kevin's help), when I needed people to stay with me so Kevin could go to work, I wasn't trusting the process. I wanted to hurry the process so I could get back to my independent self. But I didn't. Some days I did nothing more than move from the bed to the couch and back to the bed. I didn't see how I was going to get better "doing nothing," but I did what the doctor said. When he told me I could start stretching my arms, I did. When he said I could start walking more, I did. When he finally said I could drive, I did. Anyway, I guess my point is, sometimes we just have to trust the process. We may not agree with it. We probably aren't going to like it. We often want to rush it. But if we just trust the process, 99 percent of the time, it will work out. Maybe not the way we hoped it would, but it will work out.

There are so many examples in the Bible of people trusting the process. Why had I never connected this to my life before? What I was going through was no different than anyone else; it was a matter of trusting it would work out.

Take Noah for example. Noah worked on building that ark for years. He did what God told him to do. But think about the ridicule he likely received from others. Here is Noah building this massive boat and never before had it rained so hard you would need a boat. But what did Noah do? He built an ark. He trusted the process.

What about David and Goliath? Goliath was huge compared to little David. But David trusted God, and he knew the size of his obstacle didn't matter because he knew the size of his God. One stone and Goliath was defeated. David trusted the process.

Maybe the most known story in the Bible is that of Mary, the virgin who became pregnant with Jesus at the time we now celebrate as Christmas. An angel came to her and said, "Do not be afraid, Mary: you have found favor with God, you will conceive and give birth to a son, and you are to call him Jesus" (Luke 1:30–31 NIV). Mary chose to trust the process. She didn't know what exactly the process would bring or what type of reaction she would receive from others, but she trusted the process.

This world is full of hurting people. It could be sickness, failed marriages, loss of jobs, or children who have taken the wrong path. No matter what the issues are or how trivial it may seem, my hope is that they too trust the process. It's ugly, it's not fun, but when it all works out, it's amazing.

On the same day, I received the news that I could return to work. I stopped by for a surprise visit with my students. Seeing their faces light up when they saw me was something I will never forget. They were the most difficult ones to tell of my diagnosis, and now I could surprise them with my early return. It was so nice to see the fear and disbelief I saw on their faces just a few months earlier turn to huge smiles, cheers, clapping, and even some tears of joy. When I returned for work the following Monday, a pink crown awaited me. I had conquered cancer.

Next time life gets you down and your questioning "why me?", I encourage you to change your thinking to trusting the process. The process is not going to be fun. The process is probably not going to make sense. But I guarantee, if you trust the process, it will work out. Maybe not the way you hoped, but it will work out. If God puts a Goliath in your path, it's because he believes there is a David in you.

Trust in the LORD with all your heart and lean not
on your own understanding; in all your ways submit
to him, and he will make your paths straight.

—Proverbs 3:5–6 (NIV)

Think of a time you had to trust the process. Write what happened and the outcome of trusting the process. Is there something going on right now in your life where you need to trust the process?

11

THINK BEFORE YOU SPEAK

If you don't have anything nice to say, don't say anything at all!

How many times have we heard this saying? Unfortunately, it is a saying that has gone through my head so many times since my diagnosis. While I understand that most people are trying to be nice and maybe trying to cheer me up with humor, I cannot even begin to count the number of times a hurtful comment was made to me. I'm not a confrontational person, and therefore, I just let it go. But I find it necessary to talk about the importance of thinking before you speak in the hopes that I will save someone else from the sting of the comments. Words are powerful. They can have a powerful impact that is either good or bad. However, once words are spoken, they can never be taken back.

Often words can be used as motivation. I'm sure you can think of lots of times someone has said something to you and it completely made your day. Something as simple as "glad to see you today" can totally change a person's day. Is there something someone said to you that completely changed your life? Have you told that person how much what they said meant to you?

Now, if you haven't already, think about something that has been said to you that was hurtful. What was said? Do you think it was said to intentionally hurt you? I've found that often the things that seem most hurtful were never intended to be hurtful. Sometimes the person saying it doesn't even realize they hurt you. Likewise, I'm sure you can think of a time you said something to someone that hurt them, but you had no intentions of hurting them. I feel like that's what happened to me.

As I mentioned before, sometimes it's very awkward when you tell someone you have cancer. Once they have time to process the information, many opinions and suggestions start to come out. The one I heard the most was "hey, you get a free boob job now!" Well, first of all, it's not free. It cost me almost $12,000 for just the first surgery and that was after insurance, which is nowhere near free. Secondly, it cost me a lot more that doesn't have a monetary value.

It cost me a huge blow to my self-esteem. Mastectomies don't come without scars. I have horizontal scars across my chest where each breast was cut in half, the nipple removed, the breast emptied, and then sewn back together. I will never be able to look in a mirror and not see what cancer took from me.

It cost me a lifetime of worry about recurrence and spread. Most breast cancer recurrences happen in the first five years. My cousin Laura's came back in three years. I'm constantly worried about it. Will it come back? Where will it come back? Will I have warning signs next time?

It cost me a ton of physical pain. I no longer can lay flat in a bed without major pain. I have a constant ache in my left side that I can't get to go away no matter what I try. I can't move my arms correctly to be able to put on a coat without pain. I can't put both hands above my head at the same time without pain.

So, yes, I have non-saggy boobs, but I would have given anything to keep the saggy ones and not have to deal with everything cancer brings with it. I know people were trying to make light of the situation, but telling someone with cancer they are lucky because they are getting a free boob job is something you really should think long and hard about before saying it.

The second comment I heard way too much was "if I were you, I would've just stayed flat." Well, good for you, but someone in the process of recovery doesn't need your opinion at that time. The reconstruction process is not an easy process. And if I thought that was what people were meaning when they said that, I would totally understand. But they aren't saying that; they are saying they really would rather have a flat chest than have a full chest. Obviously, this is a personal choice. I would never feel differently about someone who chose to stay flat. But I don't think anything can possibly prepare you to wake up from surgery, look in the mirror, and see a man's chest. Your womanhood has been taken. You feel like everyone you see instantly looks at your chest and sees how flat it is. You feel like there is no way your husband could possibly be attracted to you anymore. You feel deformed. I'm sure many large-chested women dream of being smaller, but smaller and flat are two totally different things.

Again, I'm sure that none of the people who said this to me meant it in a hurtful manner. But it did hurt. Every time. Be careful with your words. Once they are said, they can only be forgiven not forgotten.

Set a guard over my mouth, LORD; keep
watch over the door of my lips.

—Psalm 141:3 (NIV)

Have you ever said something you later regretted? Have you ever had something said to you that hurt you greatly? Write about those experiences. How can we heal the hurt that words can cause?

12

HELLO?

My husband and I started a life group in our church shortly after my surgery. It was a group of about ten people who would meet together on Tuesday nights to discuss the past Sunday's sermon. One of our topics was on hearing God. How do we know when it's God trying to tell us something? He doesn't say, "Hey, Jill, it's me, God. Listen up!"

In the case of my cancer, I feel like God's way of speaking to me was by giving me a rash. Now, when I saw the rash, I didn't immediately think, *Oh, that's God talking to me*. My first thought was, *Great, how do I get rid of this?* It wasn't until several weeks later when I showed up for a screening mammogram and the rash mysteriously disappeared that I started thinking. Why was that rash there and wouldn't go away no matter what I tried? But then I showed up to get it checked and it disappeared! Once the diagnosis was made, it was clear to me that God and maybe my guardian angels were speaking to me through that rash. I needed something to make me go to get that mammogram done early. The rash did the trick. I was told numerous times how lucky I was to have caught the cancer so early as it was a fast-spreading type. But God didn't yell to me, "Hey, Jill, you have cancer. Go to the doctor." He did something that made me realize there was a problem and then led me to the doctors who found the cancer.

Another thing that I now know was God talking to me was at work. At the beginning of the school year, a student aide was placed in my classroom. It was just a random chance that some boys were placed in my class who needed an aide. Right before school started, I met her, Jackie Wood. We hit it off right away. I found out her son had autism, and I have a nephew very close in age who also has autism. I soon found out through our daily conversations that this was her first year being an aide or even working in a school system. She had been in the business world prior to this. She told me that last year, she was diagnosed with breast cancer. She told me all about the surgery, the hospitals, and doctors, her family history of breast cancer. Her bout with cancer caused her to reprioritize her life, and she left the business world behind. But all of this was *prior* to me knowing I had cancer. Mind you, I likely had the cancer at the time I met her, but I didn't know it. When I had the rash, I told her about it and that I was going to get a mammogram. She agreed it was good to get it checked. After that came back abnormal, she was right there to tell me what to expect next. Every step of the way, Jackie was giving me pointers, reassuring me, and checking up on me. I can't even describe how much calmer I would be after talking with her. After my diagnosis, we were talking one day and she mentioned that she wasn't even supposed to be in my room! When she was hired, she was told she was going to be working in the room next to mine, but for some reason it got changed. I know why it got changed. God did that. He needed someone to be a voice to me to make sure I went for that mammogram, someone who had recently been through it and knew all the right things to say.

I think too often we expect God's voice to be obvious. We pray to him and expect to hear his answer. But so many times, we don't realize it's God's voice until after the fact.

Your word is a lamp to my feet and a light unto my path.

—Psalm 119:105 (NIV)

When has God spoken to you before? Was it direct or indirect? Did you realize it at the time or not until after the fact?

13

INNOCENCE

Jesus loves the little children,
All the children of the world,
Red and yellow, black and white,
They are precious in his sight,
Jesus loves the little children of the world.

Do you remember singing this song as a little kid? I do, but I don't think I ever really thought about the meaning of it when I was little. It was just a song we sang in Junior Church. You might recall I mentioned that I took a position in our church as one of the Children's Coordinators just prior to being diagnosed with cancer. One of the things that our children do is write down praises and prayers for that week. So the children tell us what they would like to pray for and then they tell us anything fantastic in their life that would be a praise report.

Listening to these kids share their praise and prayer reports definitely makes you realize how much adults take for granted. Here are some examples of praise reports from kids:

I got a new puppy!
The sun was shining, and I got to play outside!
We got to have pancakes for dinner last week!

I got new socks!

My brother was nice to me yesterday!

And my personal favorite: Miss Jill, my new preschool has ukuleles! I mean, what preschool is complete without ukuleles?

What would be on your praise report? I guarantee you didn't think about thanking God for providing you with socks! Or thanking him for sunshine so you could play outside! Kids see the little details that adults often overlook.

Many years back, I was watching my two nephews before their bus came for school one day. One of my nephews is autistic. Things were a little hectic, and we couldn't find a shoe that was needed. Then we got outside and realized we forgot a book bag, so we had to run back inside to get it. Meanwhile the bus was there and ready for us. One nephew went straight for the bus, but the other one kept pulling back from me and pointing. He was saying something, but with the sound of the bus and me being anxious because we were late, I didn't have time to listen to him. Finally, he said, "Jill…did you hear me? I said listen to those birds. They are all singing. That means it's spring!" I'll be honest. I didn't hear even one bird until he mentioned it. Then, that's all I could hear. I was so focused on the fact we were late and he needed to get on that bus that I missed the delightful song of some birds, some of God's creations.

Children bring attention to the little things in life. When do we outgrow the ability to do that? When was the last time you stopped and listened to the birds sing? Or took a walk through the woods and marveled at all the animals that live there? Or went rock hunting and came home with a pocket of treasurers? Adulthood is crazy busy, but stopping to see the little things will bring some calm back into our daily lives.

Sometimes it's the little things, the small details, that mean the most to someone. My youngest stepdaughter, Emma, loves to shop with me. She also likes to mimic me. When I order a drink at a restaurant, she will often order the same thing. If I get dressed before she does, she often appears in a similar outfit. If I wear boots, she wears boots, and so on. When she was eight, she was very into birthdays. My birthday that year fell on Thanksgiving, and that was all she talked about for a month. Jill's birthday, Jill's birthday, Jill's birthday. A day I'd rather just forget about was super exciting for her. The day before my birthday, she drove me crazy, asking when her dad was going to be home from work because she wanted him to take her to the store. He finally got home and took her. She said she knew exactly what she was going to get. Although it took them several trips around the store, Kevin said they finally found exactly what she was looking for. I of course had to hide my eyes while she placed the present in front of me. I opened it up, and there was a cardinal music globe that I had looked at in the store a month or two prior. She was with me that day, and she told me, "I remembered you like cardinals, and I remembered how your eyes got watery when we listened to the music." I have always said that cardinals are a sign of my mom and my pops. I never saw cardinals until their passing, and now I see them always at the right times. Emma was only eight, but she remembered that small detail, my eyes getting watery, that told her that was something special to me. It's a gift I will always cherish for sure.

Emma went with us when I went to one of my follow-up appointments. She was seven at the time. She stayed outside with her dad while I went in for the appointment. When I got in the car she anxiously said, "So what did she say?" I told her the doctor said they got all the cancer and I was cancer-free. Her whole face lit up, and she started clapping and yelling, "Yay!" We should all have reactions like that when God answers prayers.

Next time you pray, I encourage you to think like a child. Thank God for all the little things in your life—your home, having food in your cupboard, having running water in your house, having a car to get you to work. Don't just thank him for the big answered prayers; thank him for all he does for you every day. At the same time, I encourage you to watch the little details with your friends and family. Little things mean a lot.

Truly I tell you, unless you change and become like little children, you will never enter the kingdom of heaven.

—Matthew 18:3 (NIV)

Make a list of all the things you need to praise God for. Remember the little things we often take for granted.

14

ARE YOU KIDDING?

As I mentioned earlier, I choose to have reconstruction at the same time as my mastectomy. I had never heard about reconstruction before, nor did I have any idea how it worked. Even though my surgeon explained it to me prior to surgery, it was a bit of a blur understanding what was about to happen.

Basically speaking, when you have a mastectomy, everything is taken out and you are left flat. Since I wanted reconstruction, I had an immediate second surgery to have expanders placed. The expanders look like the top part of a jellyfish. There is a magnetic part on the top which shows the doctor where the port is. When I would go into the surgeon's office, they would use a magnet over my chest to find the port. Then they would use a needle and inject 60 cc of saline per side into the expanders. The expanders then would gradually stretch my skin to get it back to a size that we could put implants in. I got these injections every week from right after my surgery until the end of February.

As the time went on, the more these injections hurt. Think of how your skin feels when it's swollen, for example, if you've ever been stung by a bee and it causes swelling. There is a tight feeling, not really painful, but super tight. That's how it felt. I was warned that the last two would be the most painful as your skin doesn't have much room to stretch. My last two injections took me 800 cc on each side. While my breasts were finally back to a decent size, they were as hard as rocks! People at work probably thought I was crazy because I would have them feel how hard it was at the top. I'm pretty sure I could've taken a bullet with those things and be fine! At the point of my last fill in February, I had been wearing a surgical bra twenty-four seven for two and a half months straight. The only time it came off was for fills or to shower.

I got my last fill the last week of February 2020. On March 13, 2020, the state of Ohio shut down because of COVID-19. Any elective surgeries were cancelled indefinitely. Doctor's offices were closed or very limited with appointments. I went for an ultrasound in April, and I was the *only* patient in the entire radiology department. I started to wonder if I was stuck with those expanders for life!

Luckily, my surgeon used a small hospital to do his reconstruction surgeries, and they opened up on a Saturday to try to catch up from the backlog created by the lockdown. I was first up on the docket for Saturday, May 30. At that time, they were allowing one person to go into the surgery center with you. A few weeks later, hospitals did not allow anyone to go in with patients. It was time to remove these hard rocks and move to something softer.

When people from anesthesiology came to talk to me, I told them to prepare for me to be super sick. I told them I vomit nonstop and even the nausea meds don't help. This surgery was outpatient, and Kevin had a bucket in the car because he knew I'd be vomiting all the way home!

The IV for this surgery was put in my foot. I've never had a foot IV before but that makes sense since they would be moving the top half of me around and my foot wouldn't be bothered during that.

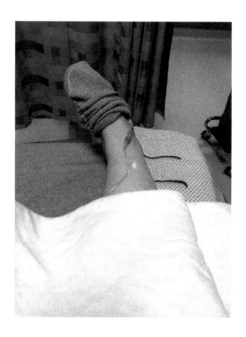

When the anesthesiologist came back, she told me that she reviewed my chart and that she was going to use a different medicine to put me to sleep. She promised that it wouldn't make me sick. Kevin and I both laughed at her because we knew how I would react to anesthesia.

I woke up in recovery and wasn't even sure they had done my surgery. I thought maybe I had just dozed off for a minute while waiting in pre-op. The nurse set my bed up and handed me some applesauce and a juice to drink and said she was going to get my husband. I felt silly asking her, but I said, "Did I already have the surgery?" She laughed and said, "Yes, honey, everything went great. We will have you wrapped up and out of here within the hour." I was so confused. I was not sick in the slightest. I drank the juice and ate the applesauce. Kevin was sitting on the side of the bed, ready to grab the vomit bucket. He kept asking if I was okay, and I kept saying "Yeah?" in almost a question rather than an answer. I was not in the least bit nauseous. Kevin was still skeptical and kept an eye on the bucket while we drove home, but I never got sick. I don't know what they used to put me under, but I will be finding out if I ever have to have surgery again. I came home with drains again, but by this time, I was a pro at them. This exchange surgery was much easier on me than the first surgery was.

Do you ever worry about something and then find out there was nothing to worry about? That's how I felt from this surgery. I was dreading it not because of the surgery but because of how sick I knew I would be for hours afterward. Then when I didn't get sick, I was confused why I didn't.

Are you a worrier? Most people are at some point in their life, but I've always envied those who never seem to have a care in the world. Worrying about things reminds me of Mary and Martha in the Bible. Jesus was coming to visit their home and Martha was busy preparing and cleaning and making sure everything would be perfect. Even after Jesus arrived, Martha continued to make everyone comfortable and worked to make food for everyone. Her sister Mary, however, sat at the Lord's feet, listening to what he had to say. Martha was upset that Mary wasn't helping her and mentioned this to Jesus. He replied simply, "Mary has chosen what is better, and it will not be taken away from her." Mary was right where she should be. She was at the feet of her guest, listening to him and giving him her attention. Meanwhile, Martha was hustling and bustling about, doing things that no one else even noticed or cared about.

Are you a Mary or a Martha? Do you invite people to your house and then spend the entire time they are there preparing, arranging, cleaning up, and putting away rather than spending quality time with them? Or are you a Mary and give your undivided attention to those who are in your presence? I realize we can't all be Marys, or there would be no food to eat and the house would be a mess, but we can take some lessons from Martha and Mary. Do what needs done, but do not miss out on quality time with those you love.

Do not be anxious about anything, but in every situation, by prayer and petition, with thanksgiving, present your requests to God. And the peace of God, which transcends all understanding, will guard your hearts and your minds in Christ Jesus.

—Philippians 4:6–7 (NIV)

Are You a Mary or a Martha?

Quickly jot down all the things you need to get done in the next ten days. Then, look back at that list and put a star beside those things that *only* you can do. (The dishes are not something *only* you can do if others live with you.) Where can you enlist help to cross something off your list so that you have more time to enjoy those around you?

15

WAIT...WHAT?

On top of not getting sick from the anesthesia, the exchange surgery was a much easier recovery than the mastectomy. The surgeon used the same incisions that were used originally. Unfortunately, the side that had cancer did not want to heal correctly the second time. I kept getting fluid buildup on that side. When the sutures came out, so did a large amount of fluid from a tiny little part that had not healed. The doctor cleaned it and put me on antibiotics, but after a few weeks, it was decided I needed to have the site opened back up, cleaned good, and stitched up.

Well, that sounded easy enough, right? I arrived for my 8:00 a.m. appointment and changed into my napkin vest as I called it. It's the same type of material as the gowns given at most doctor's offices except this was just a vest, the type that rips when you pick it up and rips even more when you try to put it on! I was taken to the procedure room and away we went.

Now, I don't know about you, but I have never been in surgery without being put under. This surgery was in the office, so there was no putting me to sleep. I'm completely numb in that area all the time now, so I wasn't worried about the pain. I was more worried about the fact that I knew in my mind that I was being cut open, and let's just say I don't do well with blood. Besides the pain, there is one distinct difference between having a procedure done while awake and one done while you are asleep. That difference would be your hearing. I could literally hear as he split my skin open with the scalpel. But what's even weirder is hearing that sound, seeing the assistant holding pressure and wiping up blood, and me not being able to feel a thing! It's like your mind and ears are playing tricks on you and saying, "Wait…what is going on?" My mind was saying, "This should hurt. He just split you open. Don't you hear that?" At the same time, my body was saying, "We don't feel anything. All is good here!" Luckily, the procedure didn't take much more than an hour, and I came out with stitches stretching across the entire incision, which is about five to six inches long. I was super proud of myself for not passing out. As you recall, I don't do well with blood (or hearing my skin being cut open!).

A few weeks later, I returned to the same office to have a checkup. I had been to that office probably twenty times between all the appointments, weekly fills, etc. Every time I went, the same lady was at the front desk and the same nurse, Megan (she's awesome), took me back and helped the surgeon with the procedures. I had never seen anyone else and assumed it was just the three of them working there.

On this visit, a new lady took me back. I was wearing a mask due to COVID regulations, as was she, but I knew I had never seen this lady before, and I knew it wasn't Megan. She greeted me saying, "It's good to see you again!" I thought that was odd, as I had never seen this lady, but I just agreed and followed her back. When we got in the room, she began taking my vitals and she said, "How are you feeling? You look a lot better than last time I saw you." Wait…what? Last time you saw me? Now I was starting to wonder who this lady was. Where would I have seen her that I wasn't feeling well or didn't look well? I again just agreed and said I was doing good, and she left the room.

A short time later, Megan and the surgeon came in. I was super glad to see Megan because like I said, she is awesome. Still feeling confused, I said, "It's good to see you, Megan. I thought maybe you had left the office because that other lady brought me back." She said, "Oh no, she just got you checked in today. I'm always here." So

I pressed on. "She acted like she knew me, but I've never seen that lady before. How long has she worked here?" Megan started laughing. She said, "Oh, she is our surgical nurse. She does all the surgeries with Dr. Z. She has seen you before, a couple times, but I doubt you remember seeing her!" Mystery solved!

Has your mind ever played tricks on you? Times where you had to stop and say, "Wait…what?" Think about some instances in the Bible when people might have said, "Wait…what?" The first one that comes to mind is Mary. An angel appeared to her and told her she was going to have a baby and she was to name him Jesus and he would be called the Son of the Most High. Wait…what? If that wasn't a "wait…what" moment, how do you think Joseph (whom she was to be married to) felt when he got this news? There are lots of examples like this—Noah when he was told to build an ark or the woman at the well, who had been divorced five times when Jesus spoke to her about her past sins but then used her to bring others to him.

And he said to them, "Why are you troubled, and why do doubts arise in your hearts?"

—Luke 24:38 (NIV)

What "wait…what" moments have you had? Did any of them change your life? If so, how?

16

EMERGENCY

As you will recall, my husband and I were married for only three months prior to my cancer diagnosis. By December of 2020, we had survived my cancer diagnosis and treatment and nine months of COVID-19. Things were finally getting back to normal and we were a happy, healthy family again. Little did I know how untrue that last statement actually was at the time.

January and February of 2021 were very snowy in Ohio. While there wasn't a lot of snow all at once, it snowed off and on for several weeks. My husband's job as a landscape designer required him to help with snow removal in the winter. He had been out plowing for numerous hours several days in a row at the end of January. I had been working from home a lot due to the road conditions that caused my school to close.

On February 2, Kevin had been out plowing since midnight. He called me in the morning to check in and said he would be home probably around noon. I told him I was getting ready to teach a class so not to call me back until after eleven thirty. Shortly after ten forty, he called. I was teaching, so I didn't answer. He called back and then sent a text that simply said "emergency." My heart sank. I was sure he had been in an accident with the plow truck. My fingers could hardly push the buttons to call him back. Nothing could have prepared me for what he was about to say to me and how my life would change at that moment.

We all have had moments when we wish we could go back and change something we said or something we did. A word or action done in a moment of anger can change a life forever. If there is one thing certain about life, it is that life changes. Look back at just your life since yesterday. What things have changed since then? What about in the last month? The last year?

There are several examples of change in the Bible—things that change people's lives in a way they would never expect—for instance, Lazarus. Lazarus was dead. He was dead for several days. Martha and Mary as well as others had mourned him, yet Jesus came and raised him from the dead. Talk about a life change! Before Jesus broke bread, thousands were famished. Suddenly, they had food to eat and their lives were changed.

There is a saying: "It's always darkest before dawn and bleakest right before the miracle." Often, we don't notice this until after things are improving. Only then can we look back and see the point when things changed. Little did Kevin and I know on February 2 that although it was dark and bleak, it wasn't even close to being the darkest or bleakest that we would experience in the coming weeks.

Many are the plans in a person's heart, but it
is the Lord's purpose that prevails.

—Proverbs 19:21 (NIV)

Have you ever received a phone call that changed your life? What was it about? How did your life change because of it?

17

THE PARKING LOT

My fingers finally got the buttons pushed, and Kevin answered on the first ring. His voice told me instantly this wasn't going to be good. He said, "I'm going to the hospital." I asked why, and he said, "I think I had a stroke. My left side is numb." This could've been one of those "wait…what?" moments. In the course of the next three minutes that I was on the phone with him, his voice slowly faded and started slurring to the point I couldn't understand him. When I would ask him where he was, he would only say "in the truck." It is impossible to call a squad for someone when you don't know where they are and also a totally helpless feeling. He did tell me that he had called a coworker who was on the way from another parking lot nearby. I prayed this was true.

Our conversation got to the point where he was barely answering me or making sound other than slurred words, and that's when I heard the voice that I will forever be grateful for. I heard someone yelling, "Kevin, Kevin, wake up. Stay with me Kevin. I'm calling the squad." Thank the Lord, Kevin did call his coworker Justin, and Justin came immediately. Justin was able to give the squad the details of his location and then relay information to me on what was going on. The only thing we really knew was that he had lost strength and feeling in his left side, his voice was slurred, and something was majorly wrong.

In February of 2020 in Ohio, there were still numerous COVID mandates. Masks were required everywhere, but hospitals also were not allowing visitors. Because of that, I was not allowed in the hospital to be with my husband or talk to a doctor. I went inside when I got to the hospital to give them my phone number and was told I would need to go back outside. Before I went out, they did tell me he was being treated for a stroke and they would call with more information.

This meant I would spend the next five hours sitting in my car in an emergency room parking lot, waiting for someone to tell me what was going on. My older brother, Jeremy, and Kevin's mom, Jeri, joined me at times as we sat and waited. After about three hours of sitting in the parking lot, I was asked to come inside to get his belongings from the nurse as he was being transferred to a Columbus hospital.

Once inside, the nurse allowed me to go in his room. He was covered in what looked like hundreds of blankets. He never opened his eyes the whole time I was in there, but he did speak a little. When I asked him if he needed anything, he just would say "I want to go home." He was not using his left side at all and had very little strength on the right side. The nurse explained to me that the tests they did were all negative for a stroke. At this point, they were feeling he had a seizure. He was being sent to Columbus for evaluation and to see a neurologist. I returned to the parking lot and waited another two hours before the transport squad came to take him to Columbus. I would not be allowed in the Columbus hospital either.

So what do you do when you can't be where you want to be or can't see who you want to see? You sit in the parking lot and pray. A lot. You call and text everyone you know and have them do the same. The word *pray* or a version of the word *pray* such as *prayer, praying, prayed*, etc. is in the Bible over four hundred times.

> Rejoice always, pray without ceasing, give thanks in all circumstances; for this is the will of God in Christ Jesus for you. (1 Thessalonians 5:16–18 ESV)

While I was praying in this situation and definitely praying without ceasing, I was not rejoicing or giving thanks. What did I have to rejoice about? What would I be giving thanks for? Thinking back later, I can answer these questions. I should have been rejoicing that Kevin was able to stop the truck when he felt odd and did not hit someone with his plow truck causing more injury. I should have been thankful that Justin got to Kevin when he did and was able to call for help. I should have been thankful that I was working from home that day and was able to get to the hospital quickly. I should have been thankful the weather had cleared enough that the roads were okay to drive on at that point of the day. But at that time, I wasn't thankful. I was in the why me or why us mode again.

> But truly God has listened; he has attended to
> the voice of my prayer. (Psalm 66:19 NIV)

Rejoice always, pray without ceasing, give thanks
in all circumstances; for this is the will of God in
Christ Jesus for you. (1 Thessalonians 5:16–18)

Think of a time that you were praying and praying and praying for something. What could you have also been rejoicing about or been thankful for at that time? Did you think about that at the time or only now? I encourage you to remember to rejoice and give thanks next time you are praying without ceasing.

19

WRONG KIND OF HOUSE

Kevin made it to the hospital he was transferred to that night, and I received word that he was in his room and being evaluated. The next morning, I called and talked to his nurse Noah. Noah could not find Kevin's cell phone, so he went to Kevin's room, got the phone number for the room phone, came back and gave me that number, and then told me to call it in five minutes. Noah then went to Kevin's room, got him awake and situated, and answered the phone when I called. He then helped Kevin hold the phone so I could talk to him. Noah is a saint!

Kevin slowly regained some strength in his left side but wasn't really improving much. They diagnosed him with epilepsy and decided to send him home. I was asked to go to the hospital to learn how to take care of him from PT. This is when I learned we live in the wrong kind of house. We live in a split-level house with bathrooms on the lower level but showers only on the top floor. We did not have grab bars in our showers/bath, nor did we have a walk-in shower. We also did not have grab bars near any of our commodes. This was going to be a challenge.

I contacted three men who were able to meet us at the house when I got home with him. He used a walker, but basically, he just dragged his left leg and stepped with his right. He didn't have a lot of strength in his arms either but enough, so he was able to somewhat hold himself up. It took some doing, but the men were able to get him in the house and down the steps. My best friend, Gretel, and her husband came and helped put handles to grab by the toilet, and he also helped me get the shower doors downstairs that I had taken off the master shower to make it a walk-in shower.

Anytime he needed to shower, we had to go up the stairs. It took me and him both to get him showered in the beginning. Since we didn't have a shower chair, we used a folding chair. We did what we could to make it work.

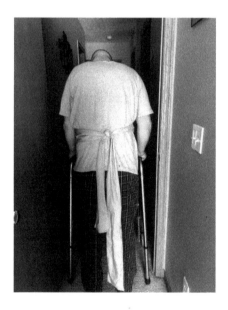

After a week, he felt like he could go to work at this desk job. The first day, he only went for part of the day. The second day, he went for the whole day, and this was a Friday.

I was supposed to pick him up at five and around 4:15 p.m., he texted and said he wanted me to look at his leg because he thought it was a little swollen and maybe purplish. It's about a thirty-minute drive home, so it was pushing 5:30 when I got home and looked at his leg. Instantly, I could tell it was swollen and definitely purple. But the biggest indicator something was wrong was when I touched his leg. It was *ice-cold*. He contemplated just laying down and putting his feet up to see if that helped the swelling. Had the leg not been so cold, I might've agreed with him, but instead, we headed back to the ER for what we thought would be a quick check and then go back home. Instead, we were in for the shock of our lives.

So you also must be ready, because the Son of Man will
come at an hour when you do not expect him.

—Matthew 24:44 (NIV)

When have you had a shock-of-your-life moment? Did it change your outlook on life? What do you do differently since having that moment?

20

DEAD BY MORNING

On Friday, February 12, I again spent about six hours in the parking lot of the hospital, waiting for Kevin to be transferred to Columbus yet again. When I helped Kevin into the ER, the nurse came around the desk to look at his leg. After one look, she instantly took him back. I took my place back in the car and waited.

I got several texts from Kevin while he was in the ER since he was coherent this time. About two hours after he arrived, he called. He told me they figured out the issue, and it wasn't good. They found multiple blood clots going from his leg to his heart. He was in serious condition. The doctor said if we had not gone to the hospital and instead let him lie down and go to sleep, he would've been dead by morning. Let that sink in.

How would you live with yourself knowing that something you allowed to happen ended up killing someone? Thousands of people live with that guilt—someone who let a friend drive drunk who ended up causing a wreck, someone who let their drug-abusing son go to a known drug house where he got drugs that had been laced and killed him. Luckily, this wasn't something I had to deal with, but it certainly made me think. What was the last thing I would have said to him before he lay down and didn't wake up?

Which brings me to my next point. You've heard a million times that tomorrow is never promised. But despite knowing that, how many times have you let someone leave in anger or left someone without telling them you loved them? It may seem routine, or like you don't have to do it every time, but what happens when that one time you don't…and you never get the chance again?

Transport finally arrived around midnight to take Kevin to Columbus. I was allowed inside to say goodbye to him before he left. During his first go-round at the hospital, he never "looked bad." He was super tired and didn't have movement of his body, but he looked like Kevin. This time, that was not the case. He was a blue ash color, and he was sweaty all over even though he said he was cold. The nurse told me he would have surgery either once he got there or early the next morning. Back home I went again while he headed to Columbus because I wasn't allowed in the hospital.

The next morning, Kevin called and was in good spirits. He said the doctor had been in and they would be checking his heart for holes (that was a little freaky to hear) and then he would let me know when the surgery would be. I didn't hear from him again for several hours. After about two hours, I had a feeling they had taken him to surgery and didn't tell me. So I started praying again. About four hours after the last time we had spoken, the phone rang with an unfamiliar number. I answered, and the man told me he was "Dr. Jolly," and he had just operated on my husband. He told me all about the number of clots they found, how they had to put in a stent, and then said, "Hey, your husband is right here, say hi!"

Kevin said hi in his half-sedated voice, and the doctor hung up. About a half hour later, Kevin texted and said I could come to the hospital. They were going to let me in because he had had surgery. I got to Riverside in record time, went through all the security details and check-ins and made it to his room around 3:00 p.m. He was still really loopy, but he knew it was me. He was apparently so loopy that he decided to rename me to "Jilly D." (He had never called me that before, but he still calls me that to this day!) He was lying on his back with his feet spread apart and higher than his head. My first thought was, *He looks like he's about to give birth!* Apparently, he felt the same way because the first thing he said was "looks like we are having a baby!"

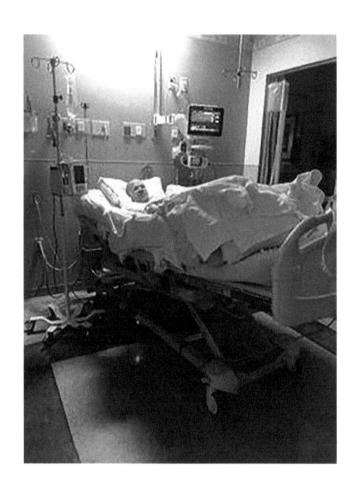

If we live, we live for the Lord; and if we die, we die for the Lord. So, whether we live or die, we belong to the Lord.

—Romans 14:8 (NIV)

We all have regrets. It's part of being human. What regrets can you just not get over? Why do you think that is? What could you have done differently? Is holding that regret helping you or hurting you? Maybe it's time to let it go.

21

THE PHONE CALL

The next day was a Sunday. Ironically, it was Valentine's Day, and our church was doing vow renewals. I joked that Kevin worked really hard to miss church, so he didn't have to marry me again! By 5:00 p.m. that day, Kevin was up and walking and ready to be dismissed. We got home just ahead of yet another snowstorm.

Monday was Presidents' Day, so I did not have to work, but I planned to return to work on Tuesday. Kevin walked in from the car on his own without assistance when I brought him home the second time, such a difference from the first time just weeks earlier. Due to the snowstorm, I ended up working from home on Tuesday as well. Kevin's mom texted me around 1:00 p.m., asking how things were going and if I was home that day. We had a brief conversation, and I went back to work.

That night, we went over the game plan again for me to go back to work the next day, hopefully for real this time. I got Kevin situated in bed and went upstairs to get stuff ready for the next day. That's when my phone rang.

Like a lot of people, my phone is used more often for texting than it is for actual phone calls. When I looked at the name on the screen, I was totally baffled. It was Bob, Kevin's stepdad. I'm not sure I've ever talked to Bob on the phone prior to that, and I wasn't even sure we had texted much. I answered knowing this was probably not a good phone call. He informed me he was at the hospital with Jeri and that it did not look like she was going to make it. Wait…what? I just talked to her hours earlier. What did he mean she wasn't going to make it? She wasn't even sick that I knew of. He then explained she had lost a lot of blood from an aortic aneurysm. They were trying to get her blood and bring her back, but it didn't look promising. He asked me to relay this information to Kevin.

That walk downstairs was the longest walk I've ever taken. I turned on the light, and he knew when he looked at me that something was wrong. I told him what Bob said and he just said "okay." I told him Bob would call back with more information. I couldn't tell if he understood what I had told him, if he was just in shock, or what type of reaction I was getting. I went back upstairs, and within about thirty minutes, the phone rang again. This time it was to tell me she was gone. I thought the walk downstairs was long the first time. Walking downstairs to tell your husband his mom just died is a *really* long walk.

It wasn't over there; the girls were both upstairs in Ava's bedroom. I went to get them and bring them downstairs with their dad so we could tell them what happened. Pure shock would be the best way to describe their reactions. That was really all of our reactions.

At this point, I was really back to questioning God again. Why was my life a constant hit of bad news after bad news after bad news? Why didn't I get to have good news for once? I headed back to work on Thursday, and that's when it started to hit me why this might be happening to me.

He will wipe away every tear from their eyes, and death shall be no more, neither shall there be mourning, nor crying, nor pain anymore, for the former things have passed away.

—Revelation 21:4 (ESV)

Have you ever had to deliver bad or shocking news to someone? What do you remember about that situation? If you had to do it again, would you do it differently?

22

TATTLETALE

Growing up, I lived on a dairy farm. We had dairy cattle, but we also had lots of barn cats. We never had an indoor cat until after I had graduated, and even then, he was an indoor/outdoor cat.

The last day of school during my first year of teaching, a student brought me a present. It was a kitten—a real, live kitten! I had every intention of keeping the cat until after school and then taking him to my grandparents' farm and letting him be a barn cat. Well, after spending the day in my classroom and a couple hours at my house that night, I couldn't go put him out to fend for himself. So Sam because my house cat. I had Sam for nineteen years!

Meanwhile, I also adopted a cat named Sadie. When Sam passed, I also adopted a cat named Quimby. Kevin always said he didn't like the cats, but I knew secretly he did. I mean, who doesn't like cats!

Emma decided she wanted a new kitten for her seventh birthday. She begged and pleaded and finally (after her birthday) her dad caved in, and little Miss Ophelia came to live with us. Even though she was pint-size, she instantly ruled the house. Quimby, who is a very large male cat, was petrified of her for a good six months of her living with us.

Despite saying he didn't want another cat and didn't like her, Ophelia could often be found lying on Kevin. She could also often be found sassing him. When he would yell at her, she would meow right back at him, looking him straight in the eye.

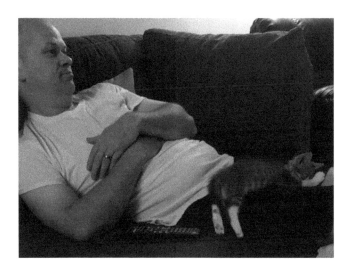

Earlier, I mentioned my mom's cat and how he seemed to have animal instinct that something was wrong when he got to the hospice floor of the hospital. When I brought Kevin home from the hospital, Ophelia would often be found lying on his left leg (the one that had the clots.)

Kevin was getting restless and was tired of my "inability" to do things the way he wanted them done, so after a few days, he tried to do stuff on his own. Some things weren't a big deal, like getting up and going into the bathroom. However, one day, I was already upstairs getting ready. The cats were in the room with me and suddenly Ophelia's head darted to the door. Then she took off down the hallway. She no sooner got to the landing and she started meowing and sassing like crazy. I knew what was happening before I even made it to her. Granted, I could also at this point hear Kevin shushing her. Kevin had come up the steps by himself, dragging his leg and all, and Ophelia was yelling at him because she knew he wasn't supposed to be doing that!

They still have a love-hate relationship, but I think it has become more of a love-love relationship even though Kevin won't admit it.

Obviously, this is an animal-owner relationship, but do you have enemies? Maybe you have people whom you call your enemies, who have no idea they are your enemy. or maybe you are an enemy to someone and you don't even know it. Back when my mom was going through her cancer treatments, I had to miss a day of work. Without going into detail, a parent wasn't happy with me for missing that particular day of work. She felt that the work I left for the sub to do was not appropriate. She called me the following day and said many choice words about the assignment, the sub, and my inability to be teacher. I explained why I was gone even though I didn't have to. I explained why the work I assigned for that day was completely appropriate even though I didn't have to. This parent continued to berate me and said she was going to the higher-ups. Needless to say, prior to the phone call, I had no idea this lady hated me so much. She did go to my principal, who in turn told her the same thing I did. The work was appropriate, and I had the right to take a sick day.

I was extremely upset about the treatment I had received and the things this woman said to me. Maybe I was a bad teacher. Maybe I shouldn't have taken the day off. Maybe I should leave the profession. I had about eighty other parents who had nothing to say about me taking a day off, but all it took was one parent to go off on me and I was second-guessing everything.

Fast forward a few years, I received my class lists and found out this parent's second child was going to be in my home base. I was instantly a mess. Should I request a change? Should I try to make amends with her? How was she going to act when she saw I was her child's teacher again?

The night of Meet the Teacher came, and I had been ready to throw up the entire day. I was so nervous. Every word she had said to me several years earlier was ringing in my head. And then, she appeared. She walked in the room with her child and was all smiles. They found her child's desk and eventually made their way to me. I braced myself as she walked up and said, "Hi, I'm _____'s mom. I don't believe we have met." *Don't believe we have met!* I've spent several years reevaluating my life because of you and you don't even remember me!

That year went perfectly, and she never once mentioned our encounter many years earlier. It was apparent she had long since forgotten it, and I had spent the last several years thinking I was her enemy and that she was out to destroy me. Maybe we shouldn't put so much merit on what others think. Maybe we should just be kind.

Love your enemies
Bless those who curse you
Do good to those who hate you
And pray for those who persecute you.

—Matthew 5:44 (NKJV)

Are you holding a grudge against someone? Do you feel someone is holding a grudge against you? Can this situation be rectified? Would it be better to reconcile, or should it remain the way it currently is?

23

I WANT TO BE LIKE...

One of my favorite things to teach when I taught social studies was advertising and persuading ads. How often do you see something on TV or see an ad and think, *I could use that*? Then, you buy it and never use it. Now what about people. Have you ever seen someone, maybe a celebrity, and thought, *I want their life*? Maybe it's not even a celebrity; maybe it's your next-door neighbor or one of your friends. However, just like the advertisements you see, you are only seeing a glimpse of this life. You are seeing the good parts, not the parts that happen behind closed doors or behind the scenes.

When I returned to work after the passing of Kevin's mom, I was standing in Denise's room, talking with some other teachers about what had been going on with Kevin. That's when I started to look at my life differently. One of them said, "I want to be you when I grow up." That's not the first time someone has said that to me. In my mind, I've always thought, *If you had any idea what goes on in my life, you would want to run the other way, not be like me.* I've asked these people why they would want to be like me, and the answers were varied but ultimately were the same. They said despite all these trials, tribulations, unexpected events, tragedies, etc., I still come to work. I don't complain (at least not often). I don't say "why me." Little do they know, I struggled big time to go to work, even to get out of bed some days. I did complain…constantly in my head and to a few select friends. I did say "why me" constantly, just not in public places and on social media. I did cry a lot, just not where anyone could see me.

Everyone deals with situations in a different way. I'm sure you can name people who never seem to have issues with their lives and those who make sure everyone knows every issue they have. I used to think people who constantly complain on social media (and in real life) or constantly are asking for prayer for this or that were looking for attention. But after thinking about how people saw my life through their eyes, versus how I saw my life through my own eyes, I realize these people probably very well feel like they are the only people who have kids who don't listen, who have health problems, who have unsupportive husbands. It's because they don't see other people talking about it. On social media, everyone's lives seem like a bed of roses. Most people don't post about every fight they have with their spouse or disagreement they have with their boss, so to others, those people's lives seem glamorous.

I got married late in life. I always thought marriage would solve a lot of issues and make me feel complete. Nope, it was a whole new world of issues I didn't even know existed because people don't talk about what happens behind closed doors. (Well, let me take that back. They don't talk about it until they are going through a divorce and then they tell every bad detail about their spouse as possible.) Who knew there is a right and wrong way to fold a towel? Who knew sixty-eight is not a desirable temperature to keep a house? Do you want to know how you find out those things? Get married!

So maybe that's why we have so many unhappy people. We as a whole need to talk more and stop comparing. People need to have others they can confide in and not have to worry about that person spreading gossip. Maybe if we talked more and shared more about our struggles, others wouldn't feel so alone. They wouldn't feel their lives are a mess based solely on what they see from the "outside looking in" of other people. No one's life is perfect no matter what they tell you.

On the same token, you never know who is watching you, simply wanting to be like you when they grow up. Kids model what they see. Being a teacher, I see this first and quite often. When parents come in for parent-teacher conferences, you often see similar mannerisms, similar facial expressions, and similar verbal phrases from these parents that you see daily with their children. Being a stepmom, I'm not really sure my stepdaughters "take after" me in anything they do. However, I was surprised to find that at Ava's fourth grade graduation, her future career goal was to be a teacher! I'd like to think that was because of me, but I don't really know if that is why she picked that. Hopefully, I'm a good role model for her and her sister.

My hope is that by reading this book, you start to look at things in your life differently. Not everything that happens to you is meant to punish you. Many times, just a change in the way we look at a situation can change our perception. Did being diagnosed with cancer stink? It sure did. Was I mad? I sure was. Did I let it define me and cry "oh poor me"? Sure didn't. Did I want to cry "oh, poor me"? I sure did.

Life is about what you make of it. Have goals and strive for those goals. Doubt kills more dreams than failure does. Believe you can do it because you can. You never know when your time will be over. During the same year Kevin had his stroke, my principal's husband was diagnosed with cancer. In just a few short months, he passed away. I was struck by what was written in his obituary. Have you ever thought about what will be said about you once you are gone? Here is a part of his:

> While Chad will be dearly missed by those who knew him, he would want everyone to know that he was prepared and eager to meet the Lord. His faith and belief were always the lantern that guided him through life. Chad, himself, stated that God had given him all he ever wanted. He said, "My entire life I prayed for a wife, a family and to be a math teacher. He provided me with everything I prayed for—I'm living the perfect life." He lived each day content and happy.
>
> Chad had a brilliant mind and a compassionate heart. Over the years as an educator, he attended many graduations. Death is a form of graduation. When we have taught all the things we came to teach, learned all the things we came to learn, then we're allowed to graduate from life. Leave it to Chad to outshine us all. He mastered all of life's lessons in only forty-six short years.

Do you live life each day happy and content? Are you working daily to graduate? I didn't graduate valedictorian or salutatorian in my class, and I'm going to guess that not many of you did either. However, we can all work to graduate as a valedictorian in life. Some of us will graduate from this life sooner than others, but one thing is certain, we will all graduate.

When my mom was told she was going to hospice care, she only broke down once. She cried and said, "I just don't want to go alone." That has stuck with me all these years. I like to think that when the time came, she didn't go alone…angels came and got her and went with her, so she wasn't alone. I recently read a story about death and what we should expect. It reminded me of my mom and what I wish I could've told her. In the story, a man tells his doctor that he is afraid to die because he doesn't know what is on the other side. He asks the doctor what he thinks. On the other side of the door they heard a dog barking and whining to get in. It was the dog of the man who was asking about death. The doctor opened the door and the dog ran inside without hesitating to his master. The doctor said, "I envision death like that. That dog has never been in this room before, but he leaped in without hesitation because he knew his master was in here. Don't be afraid to go to heaven; you know who is waiting for you there."

> There is time for everything,
> And a season for every activity under the heavens:
> A time to be born and a time to die,
> A time plant and time to uproot,
> A time to kill and a time to heal,
> A time to tear down and a time to build,
> A time to weep and a time to laugh,
> A time to mourn and a time to dance,
> A time to scatter stones and a time to gather them,
> A time to embrace and a time to refrain from embracing,
> A time to search and a time to give up,
> A time to keep and a time to thrown away,
> A time to tear and a time to mend,
> A time to be silent and a time to speak,
> A time to love and a time to hate,

A time for war and a time for peace. (Ecclesiastes 3:1–9 NIV)

There is a time for everything. If you are reading this book, you have survived everything that has been thrown at you so far in your life. Some things made you stronger, and some things may have broken you, but only temporarily. Look how far you have come. Always remember there are people who pray for you daily that you have no idea about. Remember there are people who adore you and see you as a role model that you have no idea about. Remember the person sitting beside you may be going through something you have no idea about.

As stated earlier, my cousin Laura passed from this earth in June of 2021. Her never-give-up attitude, her positivity, and her love for others is an excellent example of how we all should be. Laura's legacy has taught us six ways to live our lives.

- Speak ill of no one, for everyone is fighting a battle you know nothing about.
- Remember what happens to you doesn't define you.
- Make time for those who love you.
- Take the adventure or trip. Don't wait until a better time or until you feel better.
- Laugh often; love fully.
- Live every day to its fullest because tomorrow is never promised.

Laura fought a very courageous battle with breast cancer. Her huge celebration of life service showed the impact she had on everyone she met. If we all were to live a little more like Laura, what a different world we would live in.

The best of your life is still to come. There are people out there who are waiting to meet someone like you. There are people out there whose lives *you* will change without even realizing it. There are people who need you. There are people you have an impact on. Live each day with purpose, kindness, and compassion toward others.

You got this. Just be an overcomer!

Laura Muteti—Forever Our Hero

About the Author

Jill Dorman grew up on a dairy farm in the small town of Utica, Ohio, with her parents and three brothers. She has a graduate degree in education from The Ohio State University and a graduate degree in educational leadership from Concordia University. Jill has been an educator for over twenty years, teaching well over 1,500 students through the years.

Currently residing in Pataskala, Ohio, with her husband, Kevin, Jill has four stepchildren: Nik, Jake, Ava, and Emma. Much to the dismay of her husband, they also have three cats, Sadie, Quimby, and Ophelia. The book *Be an Overcomer...Even If You Have to Do It Several Times* was inspired by her own cancer journey in 2019 as well as the cancer journey of several of her family members. To learn more about future books and how to be an overcomer, find her group, Be an Overcomer, on Facebook.

CPSIA information can be obtained
at www.ICGtesting.com
Printed in the USA
BVHW051924131221
623918BV00013B/442